YOU DON'T WANT TO BE THE BIGGEST YOU JUST WANT TO BE THE RICHEST

18 Golden Rules for Success & Happiness

Published by Brolga Publishing Pty Ltd
ABN 46 063 962 443
PO Box 452
Torquay 3228 VIC
Australia

email: markzocchi@brolgapublishing.com.au

ISBN: 9781764077637

Printed in Australia
Cover design by Luke Harris, WorkingType Studio
Typeset by WorkingType Studio

YOU DON'T WANT TO BE THE BIGGEST YOU JUST WANT TO BE THE RICHEST

18 Golden Rules for Success & Happiness

PHILLIP KRINKER

Contents

Introduction

The idea of writing this book wasn't mine. It was suggested in June 2024 by our Global CEO, José Manuel Dias da Fonseca, and our Brazilian CEO, Ariel Couto, shortly after I announced my retirement. José Manuel encouraged me to document my professional journey and share the insights and lessons I've accumulated over the years.

At first, I wasn't particularly enthusiastic about the idea. Let's face it — the world of insurance brokerage doesn't exactly scream excitement. But as I reflected on more than four decades in the industry, I realized something meaningful: despite the challenges, the occasional monotony, and the inevitable ups and downs, I never once thought about leaving the profession. In fact, I've truly enjoyed every moment. That, I believe, is worth sharing.

So what kept me engaged all these years? The answer lies in the incredible variety — of people, products, and challenges. No two days were the same. Yes, there were difficult moments, but every career has those. What mattered was that I remained curious, committed, and fulfilled by the work I did.

I agreed to write this book on one condition: that I could include my 18 Golden Rules — principles that have guided me throughout my professional life. My aim is to share the highs and the lows, showing how these Rules helped me navigate every situation. Over the years, I've made both good and bad decisions. Some mistakes were costly — but fortunately, the good decisions far outnumbered the bad. When you make bold choices, mistakes are part of the deal. Without them, you'll never accomplish anything meaningful.

The real key is to get more things right than wrong. If you do that, you'll come out ahead.

These 18 Golden Rules aren't just for insurance brokers — they're universal principles that apply to nearly every profession. Whether you're in a completely different field or just starting out in your career, I believe these Rules can help you become not only more successful, but also happier and more financially secure.

One Rule, in particular, has stayed with me throughout my 46-year career: "You don't want to be the biggest... you want to be the richest." I learned that lesson early, when I started out in the business at the age of 18, and it has shaped my thinking ever since. I never left the industry because it consistently offered the challenges and rewards I was looking for. The lessons I've learned — as an executive and later as an entrepreneur — are relevant to any business, in any sector.

Over the course of my career, I've worked in three types of organizations: a small firm, a mid-sized company, and a large corporation. Since founding my own business in 2007, I've been profitable every year except the first — and from the second year onward, the company has consistently delivered positive results. Those results reflect the principles I've followed and now wish to share.

This book is about sharing real experiences — both the wins and the missteps — and tying each one back to a Golden Rule. That way, you can clearly connect each principle to practical, real-world situations.

While writing, I especially had young professionals in mind. My hope is that by sharing my career story, I can help light the way for others. For more experienced readers, many of these Rules may feel familiar — but I believe that revisiting core values and principles is always worthwhile.

I've had the privilege of working for two of the finest insurance brokerage firms before launching my own. Over these 46 years, I've learned something new almost every day. But one truth has always remained constant: the bottom line — net operating income and cash flow — is more important than the top line of gross or net revenues.

That's not to say the top line doesn't matter. But I've always prioritized profitability and liquidity above all else. Every initiative and every one of my Golden Rules connect to this core belief — that a company's long-term success depends on its ability to generate and preserve value.

This approach has worked for me. And through this book, I hope to share it with you — so that you, too, can experience the professional satisfaction and financial rewards I've been fortunate to enjoy.

Thank you for reading. I sincerely hope you find value in these pages, and I welcome any thoughts or feedback you may have. If my experience helps you on your own path — in business or in life — then this effort will have been well worth it.

Yours sincerely,
Phillip Krinker

Preface

It's a great honor for me to have been invited to write the preface to this book, which tells the story of the distinguished gentleman, incredible professional, and above all, great human being that is Phillip Krinker.

His history is intertwined with that of Trade Credit Insurance in Brazil as, in my opinion, he has been not only a great enthusiast but the main ambassador of the product in the country.

I met Phil, as he is known by everyone, nearly 10 years ago, when I was working for an international insurer, and he was leading CredRisk – the broker responsible for issuing the very first Trade Credit policy with that insurer. Two characteristics impressed me greatly about Phil: his enthusiasm for Trade Credit Insurance and his restlessness, always seeking the new, be that product improvements or ways to increase its penetration in the Brazilian market.

Always with an optimistic, sometimes even romantic view of the topic, balanced with his natural pragmatism, Phil has been the key figure developing this market in Brazil, along with many of the professionals working in it – as identifying and developing young talent has always been one of his key focuses.

As you read the pages ahead in this book, which covers his history, his golden rules, and many of the decisive moments where he had the courage to make decisions essential for success, it is clear that Phil meticulously planned each step and phase of his life – leading up to the present day and his retirement. Great news for his wife, Ligia, who will now be able to enjoy his daily company. Not so good news for the market, which will miss the contributions of this icon. And sad for me and all my colleagues at MDS, who will miss his everyday presence.

Phil, thank you for your trust in MDS and in me, as you entrusted us with your masterpiece, your fifth child – as you refer to CredRisk! It was an honor to have you with us over the last three years. Be very happy in the fourth phase of your life, which you are of course about to begin!

With affection, Ariel

Ariel Couto - MDS Brazil CEO and Brokerslink

Americas Regional Manager

Chapter One

Golden rule # 1
You don't want to be the biggest... you want to be the richest

My insurance brokerage career began at the age of thirteen. Yes, you read that right — thirteen!

I was incredibly fortunate to meet Mr. Royal Hubert Weller and his wonderful wife, Elenor, at a young age. Every Sunday afternoon, Roy and El would "adopt" my brother and I, taking us to play golf at our country club. Back then, young children couldn't secure a tee time unless they were accompanied by adults. Roy and El were those essential adults who made it possible for us to enjoy the course.

During our many golf games, Roy would often remind me that one day, when I grew up, I was destined to become an insurance broker. At thirteen, I had no idea what an insurance broker did!

When I turned 18, Roy reached out to me and offered me an internship alongside three other trainees. My insurance career was officially taking off.

In my eyes, Roy was unquestionably the best role model and insurance broker I ever encountered. He was the CEO of Adams & Porter in Brazil, a New York-based family business founded in 1907 by Mr. Adams and Mr. Porter.

Golden rule # 4
Be a gentleman[1]

Roy was sent to Brazil in 1947 at a young age, shortly after leaving the US Marines, with the mission of managing one of Adams & Porter's largest and most important clients, Anderson Clayton. Anderson Clayton, which later became part of Unilever, had established itself in Brazil to trade in cotton and needed a local broker. Mr. Adams hired Roy in New York and sent him to Brazil to service the account locally.

These trading transactions required the expertise of a marine insurance broker to ensure that shipments from Brazil to the US were fully insured. Roy was the man for the job.

1 Dear Reader, in this Golden Rule, I refer to Mr. Royal Hubert Weller and use the word "gentleman" in his honor. I warmly invite you to embrace the spirit of this rule as one that equally celebrates "ladies" — for it's essence knows no gender, only character and grace.

At the time, Roy realized he was the only foreign insurance broker in town. Seizing this unique opportunity, he began knocking on the doors of other US and European multinational businesses that had started arriving in Brazil after World War II. Roy built a stellar reputation within the expat business community, distinguishing himself from local brokers. He spoke both English and Portuguese, upheld impeccable business ethics, and was a shrewd administrator, all of which made him the most sought-after broker in Brazil. Roy became a millionaire at a very young age!

The motto "You don't want to be the biggest... you want to be the richest" was something Roy instilled in me from the start. He was obsessed with maintaining high standards of service, good manners, reliability, and punctuality, and was one of the most ethical businessmen I have ever worked with in my 40-plus years in the industry. Roy was a true gentleman. So here's my first golden rule for business success: Be a true gentleman — everyone wants to work with a gentleman.

The second valuable tip I learned from Roy was to have initiative and differentiate yourself from the competition. Roy was in a unique position as the only foreign insurance broker in Brazil in 1947, and he capitalized on this. He impressed his peers in the expat community, bringing in huge accounts instead of just focusing exclusively on the

Anderson Clayton account. He went above and beyond his mission from his superiors in New York, leveraging the Anderson Clayton account many times over, becoming a tremendous financial and professional success.

He didn't procrastinate; he went out and secured significant accounts that he didn't necessarily need to, but did so anyway, and was handsomely rewarded for his initiative.

Roy recognized the unique opportunity he had to offer his services to other US and European companies, as the major brokers hadn't yet arrived in Brazil. He was alone, swimming in a vast sea of opportunities!

Roy found a niche and exploited it magnificently. I took this example to heart, applying it several times throughout my career. Some of these unique opportunities provided me with great satisfaction and financial reward, and I'll share more of these stories further along in this book.

I joined Adams & Porter in 1978 at the age of 18. I was determined to become the best insurance broker in Brazil and decided to focus on my formal and informal training.

To achieve this, I needed a clear career plan.

Career planning: a structured approach to success

One of the most valuable decisions I made early in my career was to approach it with a structured plan. By dividing my professional journey into four distinct phases, I was able to set clear objectives for each stage, ensuring that I remained focused, motivated, and aligned with my long-term goals. This structured approach to career planning provided a roadmap that guided my decisions and actions, ultimately leading to the success and fulfillment I've experienced.

Phase I - Schooling: laying the foundation

The first phase of my career, like most people, was spent in school. From childhood through young adulthood, the primary focus was on education — building the foundational knowledge and skills that would serve as the bedrock for everything that followed. These early years are crucial, not just because of the formal education received, but because they shape your approach to learning, your curiosity, and your work ethic. During this time, it's important to cultivate a love for learning and to develop the discipline needed to succeed academically.

While this phase may seem straightforward, it's essential to recognize that the habits and attitudes you develop during your schooling will carry over into your professional life. Embrace this time as an opportunity to explore different subjects, discover your passions, and begin thinking about the direction you want your career to take.

In today's competitive world, earning a university degree, an MBA, or even a PhD is often seen as a prerequisite for being considered a "high potential" in a major corporation. But I have some encouraging news for those who don't see themselves as top students. Over my 40-plus-year career — spanning major corporations and family-owned businesses — I've seen firsthand that many highly successful executives and entrepreneurs built their careers without even completing high school. This proves that a lack of formal education should never be seen as a barrier to success.

Success in business depends on a broad range of skills that go far beyond academic performance. Interpersonal abilities, creativity, resilience, adaptability — these traits often matter more than a flawless academic record. If you excel in these areas, you have every chance of building a successful career and achieving financial independence, regardless of your educational background. The key is to develop the mental strength to pursue your educational goals with discipline — whether that means striving for top grades or simply earning your degree. But just as important is to recognize that academic excellence is not the only route to success. Throughout my career, I've had the privilege of working with some of the wealthiest entrepreneurs in Brazil — many of whom had little formal education. Their success came from sharp business instincts, innovative thinking, and strong relationship-building skills. In this book, I'll explore those qualities through my 18 Golden Rules — a practical guide for those who may not follow the traditional path, but who have the ambition and drive to achieve great things. Embrace who you are. Your path may be different, but it can be just as rewarding.

Phase II - Learning a profession: becoming an expert

The second phase of my career, from age 20 to 40, was dedicated to mastering my profession. This is the time when you immerse yourself in your chosen field, absorbing as much knowledge and experience as possible. For me, this meant diving deep into the insurance and business worlds, with the primary goal of outlearning my peers. The emphasis during this phase was not on making money but on becoming the best in my field.

I worked in the office during the day and attended university at night to earn my BA in business. This dual commitment allowed me to gain practical experience while also advancing my formal education. The decision to study at night was particularly advantageous because it meant I didn't have to sacrifice four years of my "day" life to obtain my degree. Instead, I could continue building my career while pursuing my education, maximizing the use of my time.

Beyond earning my degree, I took at least fifteen to twenty specialization courses in various subjects, including marketing, finance, law, and insurance. I approached this phase with the mindset of a sponge, eager to soak up as much knowledge as my brain could handle. The goal was to build a comprehensive understanding of my profession, laying the groundwork for future success.

This phase is about more than just accumulating knowledge; it's about developing expertise and establishing yourself as a credible professional in your industry. It's the time to experiment, take risks, and learn from your experiences. The more you invest in learning during this phase, the better equipped you will be to capitalize on opportunities in the next stage of your career.

Phase III - Time to make money: capitalizing on expertise

From the ages of 40 to 60, I entered the third phase of my career, which I describe as the time to make real money.

By this point, I had spent two decades mastering my profession, and it was time to reap the financial rewards of that hard work. During this phase, I transitioned from being a well-paid executive to becoming an entrepreneur. This shift was significant because it allowed me to leverage the knowledge, skills, and networks I had built in the previous phase to create wealth.

It's important to emphasize that this phase is not just about making money for the sake of it; it's about achieving financial security and freedom. For me, entrepreneurship was the path that brought the most fun at work and the most financial success. However, I recognize that not everyone is cut out to be an entrepreneur, and that's perfectly fine. If you choose to remain an executive, your goal should be to become the highest-paid within your organization, maximizing your income potential during these critical years.

This phase is where the stakes are higher, and the pressure to succeed increases. You're no longer just building your expertise — you're expected to deliver results, create value, and drive growth, whether for your own business or within the company you work for. The key to success in this phase is to apply everything you've learned, remain focused on your financial goals, and be strategic about the opportunities you pursue.

Phase IV - Reaping the rewards: enjoying the fruits of your labor

The final phase of my career, from age 60 to 80, is about reaping the rewards of the hard work and dedication I put in during the previous phases. This is a time to truly enjoy life, explore new endeavors, and possibly shift focus to areas unrelated to the work I've done over the past 40 years. It's a phase of change, new experiences, and moving forward.

After decades of building, learning, and growing, this phase is about taking a step back to reflect on your achievements and savor the fruits of your labor. It's a time to invest in personal passions, spend more time with family and friends, and pursue activities that bring you joy and fulfillment. Whether that means traveling, engaging in philanthropy, mentoring the next generation, or exploring hobbies you never had time for before, this phase is about creating a life that you enjoy and that reflects your values.

It's also a time to give back. With the experience and wisdom you've accumulated, you can make a meaningful impact by sharing your knowledge with others — whether through mentoring, writing, or volunteering. This phase is not just about personal enjoyment; it's about leaving a legacy and contributing to the success and well-being of others.

Now that I've retired, I've chosen to dedicate a meaningful portion of my time to philanthropic work that reflects my personal values and life experiences. My primary focus is on supporting young children and underserved elderly communities — groups that often face significant challenges, yet possess tremendous potential and wisdom. Engaging in this work has given me a renewed sense of purpose, reinforcing my belief that giving back is one of life's most rewarding endeavors.

That said, the journey to discovering one's purpose is deeply personal. It's important for each individual to reflect on their passions, values, and the causes that truly inspire them. Through this kind of introspection, you can uncover what resonates most deeply with you and what drives you to make a difference.

Pursuing activities that align with your values not only brings meaning to your own life but also strengthens your connection to others and to the broader community. As you explore your own sense of purpose, consider the kind of impact you want to make in the world. This might take the form of volunteering, mentoring, or supporting initiatives that uplift those in need. Always remember: purpose is not a fixed destination, but a lifelong journey. It evolves as you grow, learn, and engage with the world around you. When you dedicate your time and energy to causes that ignite your passion, you create a lasting impact — not just in the lives of others, but in your own as well.

In the end, this journey toward purpose can bring a deep and lasting sense of fulfillment, enriching your life in ways you may have never imagined.

A career path for success

The four-phase career path I've outlined may seem like a lot of hard work — and it is. But for most people, a successful career will likely follow a similar trajectory. It's about recognizing that different phases of life require different focuses and that by planning ahead, you can maximize your potential at each stage.

This structured approach to career planning is not about rigidly adhering to a specific timeline but about understanding the natural progression of a career and making intentional choices that align with your goals and values. It's about being proactive, setting clear objectives, and continuously evaluating your progress.

Of course, not everyone will follow this exact path. Some, like Bill Gates, may achieve extraordinary success early in life and take a different route. But for most of us, a career is a long-term journey that requires careful planning, dedication, and the ability to adapt to changing circumstances.

By embracing this four-phase approach, you can ensure that you make the most of each stage of your career, building a foundation for long-term success and fulfillment. Whether you're just starting out or already well into your career, it's never too late to apply these principles and take control of your professional journey.

Coaching and mentoring: the power of guidance

In the fast-paced and often challenging world of business, it can be easy to lose sight of your long-term goals amid the demands of daily tasks. This is why I strongly recommend that all professionals regularly consult with a coach or mentor. Having someone to guide you, offer perspective, and hold you accountable can make a significant difference in both your personal and professional development.

The role of a coach or mentor

A coach or mentor is more than just an advisor; they are trusted confidants who can provide you with the support and guidance needed to navigate your career. The value of having someone who is not directly involved in your day-to-day work cannot be overstated. This external perspective allows your coach or mentor to offer unbiased advice, helping you see situations more clearly and make better decisions. Throughout my career, I've always had a coach who worked with me weekly. This regular interaction was invaluable in ensuring that I stayed on track with my personal career goals and, later, with the objectives of my company. A coach provides structure and discipline, helping you to set realistic goals, develop strategies to achieve them, and monitor your progress over time. This ongoing relationship fosters continuous improvement and helps you maintain focus on what truly matters.

I must take a moment to express my deep gratitude to my longtime coach and mentor, Richard Barczinski. By a remarkable coincidence, Richard had been coached and mentored by my father, Ray Krinker, years earlier. Later in life, when Richard retired as CEO of a prominent Brazilian multinational, I eagerly seized the opportunity to ask him to become my coach and mentor.

For the past 10 years, I've had the privilege of learning from him. Our relationship has become incredibly special to me, and I credit Richard with much of my professional success. In many ways, he represented a continuation of the mentoring I received from my first and greatest coach of all — my father. I consider myself extraordinarily fortunate to have shared so many hours of "father and son time" while my father was alive.

He was deeply respected in the São Paulo business community and served as a senior partner at PricewaterhouseCoopers, specializing in Mergers & Acquisitions. Over the course of 40 years with the firm, he built a remarkable career — yet he always made time for me, ensuring I was on the right path from the very start of my professional journey at the age of 18. I vividly remember our daily commutes through São Paulo's busy traffic, soaking up the invaluable wisdom he shared — insights that clients paid dearly for, yet which I received freely and lovingly. I am eternally grateful to my father and mother, who have been the best role models anyone could ever hope for.

Everything I am today is a reflection of the values and lessons they instilled in me.

Golden rule # 5
Work harder on yourself than on your job

I worked at Adams & Porter (A&P) from 1978 to 1994. At the time, A&P was widely recognized as the best broker in Brazil. It was rare to hear of A&P losing an account to the competition, an impressive record that left a lasting impression on me. The client was "king" and was treated as such, which explains why A&P lost very few clients during my tenure.

The first two years of my insurance career were spent in the auto and personal lines department. I remember sitting at a corner desk with a manual calculator, calculating thousands of auto premiums every month. It was perhaps the most monotonous job in the world, but it demanded discipline and concentration to ensure we delivered accurate premiums to clients on time.

Back in the '70s, computers were scarce in the Brazilian insurance market. Today, this work would be done by computers — faster, cheaper, with fewer people, and fewer mistakes. Although I moved on to more sophisticated lines of insurance in later years, those two years working in auto insurance proved invaluable a decade later when I secured a major auto insurance deal. This deal required the creation of an online telemarketing operation capable of handling approximately 360,000 auto insurance policies a year with just 40 employees. It was extremely innovative for the time and remained profitable for many years.

As I mentioned earlier, I was in the learning phase of my life, and my goal was to complement my day job with as many insurance and business courses as I could manage at night. This meant working during the day and studying at night. My curiosity to learn new types of insurance was insatiable.

I vividly recall when private health plans first began to be offered by insurance brokers in Brazil. In the '70s, private health plans were not regulated by the Superintendency of Insurance (SUSEP), and brokers were prohibited from selling them to clients.

I was one of the few brokers in our company to closely follow the opening of the private health insurance market. When General Accident (which later became Royal Sun Alliance and today is known as Sura, in Brazil), Cigna, Chubb, and AIG launched their private health plans in Brazil, I was among the first brokers to truly invest my time in this new line of insurance. It was an easy sell; my clients trusted my advice, and they were frustrated with the poor service offered by existing health plans, which were not considered insurance at the time.

Back then, private health plans were more affordable than they are today, and commission levels were extraordinarily high, so my commission revenues skyrocketed year after year. No one could quite understand what I had achieved.

It didn't take long for other brokers in the company to catch on, and they too began to profit by selling private health plans to their existing clients.

This experience is a prime example of using creative initiative and being the first to capitalize on new ideas. The golden rule of doing things differently (# 8) and trusting my instincts paid off.

By the age of 30, I was made a senior account executive and was given twenty clients to manage. I remember Roy coming into my office and telling me that he would return in a year to see how much I had increased my revenue stream. On average, my revenues grew by double digits each year, and in a short period I had expanded my client base from 20 to 120. As a result, I needed to grow my service team to handle the increased volume of business. This marked the beginning of my learning curve, transitioning from a pure "manager" to a "manager and leader." These two business qualities are very different and essential to understand. Anyone who aspires to be a successful businessperson must excel at both management and leadership. I'll delve deeper into this topic later in the book.

Golden rule # 6
The power of networking in expanding your client portfolio

In the landscape of business development, one golden rule stands out: to expand your client portfolio effectively, you must prioritize networking. While technical knowledge and industry expertise are undeniably important, the reality is that relationships play an equally crucial role in generating new business. The adage "it's not just what you know, but who you know" rings true in every sector, and embracing this principle can lead to significant growth opportunities.

Throughout my career, I have actively engaged with chambers of commerce and social clubs, recognizing these platforms as fertile ground for cultivating new leads. These organizations provide a unique environment where professionals from diverse backgrounds come together, sharing insights and opportunities. By attending events, participating in discussions, and building genuine connections, I have consistently found that the relationships fostered in these settings often translate into valuable business opportunities. Each handshake, each conversation, and each collaboration can open doors that might otherwise remain closed.

In today's digital age, the landscape of networking has evolved dramatically. While traditional methods remain effective, digital marketing has emerged as an indispensable tool for acquiring new clients. Social media platforms, professional networking sites, and online forums have revolutionized how we connect with others. They allow us to reach a broader audience, showcase our expertise, and engage with potential clients in real time. However, despite the efficiency and reach of digital marketing, we must not underestimate the profound impact of personal relationships. The trust built through face-to-face interactions often leads to stronger partnerships and long-term client loyalty.

My time at Adams & Porter provided an invaluable training ground that underscored the importance of both technical skills and interpersonal relationships. Over the course of sixteen years, I honed my ability to service clients and gained a wealth of knowledge in the insurance and business sectors. This experience laid a strong foundation upon which I built my career. Yet, as I developed my skills and expanded my understanding of the industry, I began to feel the constraints of my environment. The realization that I had outgrown the company was both daunting and liberating.

Stepping out of my comfort zone was not an easy decision. It meant leaving behind a familiar space where I had flourished and venturing into the unknown.

However, I understood that remaining stagnant would hinder my growth and limit my potential. Embracing change is essential in a fast-paced business world where adaptability is key. By making the bold choice to seek new opportunities, I opened myself up to a world of possibilities that aligned more closely with my evolving aspirations.

As I moved forward, I took with me the lessons learned at Adams & Porter — the technical expertise, the client service skills, and the significance of networking. Each of these elements is intertwined; while technical skills can help you land a client, it is often the relationships you cultivate that keep them coming back. The art of networking is about building trust and rapport, creating a community of advocates who believe in your abilities and are willing to refer you to others.

In conclusion, as you embark on the journey of expanding your client portfolio, remember that networking is not merely a strategy, but a vital part of your professional identity. Engage actively with your community, leverage digital tools, and nurture the relationships you build. By doing so, you will not only generate new business but also cultivate a network that supports your ongoing growth and success. Embrace the power of connection, and let it propel you toward new horizons.

Chapter Two

Golden rule # 2
Successful managers must be lazy and intelligent

Leaving Adams & Porter was a tough decision for me, especially given my strong relationship with Roy Weller. However, we both knew it was the right choice.

Today, the insurance brokerage industry is dominated by three large global players. But back in the 90s, when I decided to leave A&P, there were several excellent firms to choose from. One that intrigued me was Alexander & Alexander (A&A), represented in Brazil by Mr. Alastair Macfarlane. A&A was a joint venture between Alastair, who held 50% of the shares, and A&A USA, which owned the other 50%.

I decided to reach out to Alastair directly. Before I could finish my sentence, Alastair, a Scotsman, invited me for a drink. We met at a bar, and before I could even articulate my thoughts, he asked how much I wanted to earn, and within five minutes, the deal was closed.

Within a week, I received my formal work contract with A&A Brazil and was set to start the following Monday. Upon my arrival at the new office, my personal assistant was waiting for me in the parking lot to escort me to my new office. What a welcome! Remarkably, my personal assistant from 1994 is still with me today, marking a thirty-year professional relationship. Although she no longer comes into the office, she handles all my personal affairs with the utmost competence and trust. I will never forget all she has done for me over the years, and I am immensely grateful for her efficiency and patience.

Now, back to A&A. On my first day at work, Alastair called me into his office, which was right next to mine, and handed me a round-trip, business-class ticket to New York. "Phil, you've got to go to New York this week to be interviewed by the A&A guys."

"Interviewed? For what?" I asked.

Alastair replied, "I forgot to mention that the Chief Commercial Officer (CCO) position in the JV agreement is an A&A nomination. Phil, don't worry — you'll do fine in the interviews. I have full confidence in your interview skills." I wasn't sure where Alastair's confidence came from, considering I had only had one job interview before, and that was at the age of 13 on a golf course!

So, off to New York I went, theoretically unemployed, having handed in my resignation at A&P, with a new work contract signed by Alastair, but not yet by Alexander & Alexander.

I underwent a battery of interviews in New York, and by the end of the day, I was confirmed as the new Chief Commercial Officer for A&A in Brazil! I was even designated as a statutory shareholder of A&A, holding a few shares in the company.

The move from Adams & Porter to Alexander & Alexander was a significant step. A&P was an excellent mid-sized brokerage house, while A&A was one of the largest insurance brokerage companies in the world, with thousands of employees and extensive resources to manage large corporate accounts. It was a lot to take in, and I had to adapt quickly.

The first and most important change for me was the intensive use of technology. Technology was beginning to take off in the insurance industry in Brazil, and A&A were pioneers in this area. Alastair was the driving force behind the company's technological advancements. I attended many meetings where Alastair would often declare, "Successful brokers must be lazy and intelligent." What he meant was that we needed to leverage technology to our advantage — to reduce costs, improve performance, enhance the quality of our work, and refine our management controls and ratios, such as revenue per employee and profitability, by replacing manual processes with information technology. Alastair's phrase, "Successful brokers must be lazy and intelligent," is essentially a call for continuously improving Best Practices.

The adoption of personal computers and servers began to replace the massive and expensive mainframes. Alastair was quick to invest in this new technology, putting us miles ahead of the competition. It didn't take long for other brokers to follow suit, but Alastair remained ahead of the game.

Another important lesson I learned from Alastair was that brokers must be available 24 hours a day. Back in the early 90s, when I joined A&A, mobile phones were just coming into fashion, and having a mobile phone in Brazil was exorbitantly expensive and reserved for a select few.

Alastair gave me a mobile phone on my first day of work. At that time, I had just finished building a beautiful house in a gated community on the outskirts of São Paulo, so Alastair installed an antenna and a hands-free receiver in my car so we could chat on the way to the office and back home every day. Alastair would call me at all hours — day and night! I don't think Alastair slept much at night because he would often call me very late to discuss an idea that had popped into his head.

Alastair was the hardest-working person I have ever met. He was always on the go. I think he may have overdone it with hard work, but he was an exemplary figure when it came to dedication and achieving great results.

I am proof that hard work pays off. When Alastair decided to sell his 50% shareholding to A&A and retire, I was the one entrusted by headquarters to transfer the funds related to the sale of the shares from the company's bank account to Alastair's private account. That fund transfer was a life lesson I will never forget.

I was 34 when I joined A&A, still very much a "sponge" when it came to learning anything related to insurance or business.

Golden rule # 7
Keep ahead of the market

I recall a three-month business trip to the US where I visited the principal A&A offices in the country. I started in the main office in New York and then traveled to Chicago, Houston, Atlanta, and Miami before returning to São Paulo. During those three months, I met many knowledgeable professionals, and upon returning to Brazil, I prepared a SWOT (Strengths, Weaknesses, Opportunities and Threats) analysis of 27 different types of insurance and insurance services that we could potentially replicate in Brazil.

Not all the products and services I brought back to Brazil were successful, mainly because we lacked insurers willing to underwrite the business. However, a few were implemented in Brazil and continue to be successful to this day.

New insurance products & services

Some of the products and services that I recall being successful in Brazil include Casualty Loss Control Services, Crisis Management, Kidnap & Ransom Insurance, Reps & Warranties (M&A), Directors & Officers (D&O) Insurance, and Trade Credit Insurance.

Centers of influence: unlocking new opportunities

In my professional journey, one of the pivotal concepts that I encountered in the US was the idea of "Centers of Influence" (COIs). These individuals are not just well-connected; they are highly successful executives and entrepreneurs whose extensive networks can generate significant and profitable accounts for an organization.

The strategic importance of COIs cannot be overstated; they serve as conduits to lucrative opportunities, opening doors to large corporations around the globe.

Centers of Influence typically hold influential positions within their industries and are often invited to join a company's board or take on honorary roles. Their primary function is to leverage their relationships to foster new business opportunities. At Alexander & Alexander (A&A), for instance, the COIs were instrumental in bringing in new accounts, which significantly contributed to the company's growth. Their presence not only enhanced our credibility but also provided invaluable insights and introductions that would have otherwise taken years to cultivate.

The impact of these relationships was particularly evident during the 1996 acquisition of A&A by Aon Corporation. This merger was a transformative event that catapulted Aon into the ranks of the top three global brokers almost overnight. For A&A's shareholders, the acquisition represented a lucrative opportunity, merging the "old blue blood" of A&A with Aon's "new blood." This fusion of traditional expertise with innovative approaches created a powerhouse in the industry, setting the stage for future growth and success.

However, significant changes such as this can lead to shifts in leadership and organizational structure. In this case, the acquisition resulted in the retirement of Alastair, a key figure in A&A's leadership. This highlights an essential truth in corporate environments: change can occur rapidly and unexpectedly, compelling executives to reassess their career trajectories. It is crucial to embrace such transitions rather than resist them. My advice to colleagues and friends has always been to align with the new company's vision once an acquisition is finalized. Loyalty to the new organization and a commitment to making the merger successful can open doors to fantastic career opportunities that may not have existed before.

Reflecting on my time with both A&A and Aon, I cherish the projects and initiatives I was a part of during this transformative era. Collaborating with COIs and leveraging their networks enabled us to embark on innovative ventures that would shape the future of the company. Engaging with these influential figures not only enriched my professional life but also provided a deeper understanding of the industry's dynamics.

In conclusion, Centers of Influence are invaluable assets in any organization. They are the bridges to expansive networks and significant business opportunities. Understanding how to cultivate and maintain these relationships can profoundly impact your career and the success of your organization. As the business landscape continues to evolve, the ability to navigate changes, embrace new partnerships, and leverage the power of COIs will remain essential for long-term success. Ultimately, the relationships we build today can lead to the breakthroughs of tomorrow, transforming challenges into opportunities for growth and innovation.

Golden rule # 8
Differentiate yourself from the crowd

Differentiation is not just a strategy; it's a necessity in today's competitive market landscape. When every company is vying for the same clients, services, or market share, standing out becomes the key to survival and success. In the insurance brokerage industry, where products and services can often appear homogeneous, carving out a unique position is crucial. This is especially true when market conditions shift dramatically, as they did during Brazil's era of privatization under President Fernando Henrique Cardoso.

The birth of the privatization department

The idea of establishing a "Privatization Department" was born from a clear understanding of the market's evolving dynamics. As Brazil embarked on its ambitious privatization program, the need for sophisticated insurance solutions became evident. State-owned companies transitioning to private ownership required a different approach to risk management. These were not merely business transactions; they were complex, large-scale infrastructure projects that demanded specialized knowledge and expertise. Recognizing this gap in the market was the first step in differentiating the brokerage firm from its competitors.

The privatization of Brazil's infrastructure sectors — railroads, highways, ports, airports, energy and water utilities, and iron and steel mills — created a fertile ground for innovation in the insurance market. Traditional insurance solutions were inadequate for the complexities of these newly privatized industries. By establishing a dedicated department, the firm positioned itself as a pioneer in addressing these needs, providing tailored solutions that no other firm could offer at the time.

Leveraging expertise for market leadership

To ensure the success of this initiative, I sought out and hired three of the best engineers available. Their technical expertise was instrumental in understanding the unique challenges and risks associated with these large-scale projects. This move was more than just a strategic hire; it was a commitment to delivering unparalleled value to our clients. By integrating engineering expertise with insurance solutions, we could offer a comprehensive service that addressed both the technical and financial aspects of risk management.

This approach not only differentiated us from our competitors but also established us as leaders in a niche market. While other firms continued to offer generic insurance products, we were able to provide specialized services that directly met the needs of our clients in the privatization market. Our focus on this niche allowed us to build a reputation for excellence and reliability, attracting more clients and securing our position as the go-to firm for privatization-related insurance.

The results of differentiation

The success of the Privatization Department was evident in the results we achieved. By being the first to market with a dedicated focus on privatization, we were able to capture a significant share of the new business opportunities that arose. Our ability to offer specialized, high-quality services at a time when they were most needed set us apart from the competition.

This experience underscores the importance of differentiation in business. It's not enough to offer what everyone else is offering; you must find a way to provide something unique and valuable that meets the specific needs of your target market. In doing so, you create a competitive advantage that is difficult for others to replicate.

Lessons learned

The success of this venture taught me several key lessons about differentiation:

1. **Identify market gaps:** Successful differentiation starts with understanding the market and identifying unmet needs or opportunities. By focusing on the emerging privatization market, we were able to carve out a unique niche for our services.

2. **Invest in expertise:** Differentiation often requires investment in specialized knowledge or skills. Hiring engineers with the expertise to address the technical challenges of privatization projects allowed us to offer a service that no other firm could match.

3. **Focus on value:** Differentiation is not just about being different; it's about being better. By providing tailored, high-quality services that addressed the specific needs of our clients, we were able to build a reputation for excellence.

4. **Be first to market:** Timing is critical in differentiation. By being the first firm to establish a department dedicated to privatization, we were able to capture a significant share of the market before our competitors even recognized the opportunity.

These lessons are not just applicable to the insurance industry; they are universal principles that can be applied to any business seeking to stand out in a crowded market. By focusing on these principles, any company can differentiate itself and achieve lasting success.

In conclusion, differentiating yourself from the crowd is about more than just offering a unique product or service; it's about understanding the market, investing in the right expertise, and delivering exceptional value to your clients. When done correctly, it can lead to significant competitive advantages and long-term success, as demonstrated by the success of our Privatization Department during one of the most transformative periods in Brazil's economic history.

Golden rule # 9
Be persistent — never give up and fight to the end

A memorable story from this time involves our bid for one of the largest railroad networks in Brazil. The challenge was that we had no local expertise in railroad risks, as the Brazilian government traditionally self-insured these risks rather than purchasing insurance.

At that time, A&A was one of the largest railroad insurance brokers globally, with its center of expertise located in Philadelphia, US. When I reached out to them for support in our bid, I was politely told they were too busy to assist. However, they directed me to our colleagues in London, who had recently won the British Rail privatization bid. The response from London was similar, but I did manage to obtain a copy of the winning proposal submitted to British Rail. Using that proposal as a model, I adapted it to fit the

Brazilian context and submitted a comprehensive bid with full terms and conditions.

On the day of the presentation in Rio de Janeiro, I was surprised to see five of my top competitors waiting in the reception room. Our proposal had been sent ahead of time, and I was the last to present. Each of my competitors spent about fifteen minutes pitching their proposals behind closed doors.

When it was my turn, I humbly apologized for our non-binding indication, explaining that we lacked experience in the railroad industry and had relied entirely on our London office for the presentation of our non-binding terms and conditions. After I finished, I was asked to leave the room and wait in the reception area.

When I returned to the reception room, I noticed that all of my competitors had left — a promising sign. After about half an hour, I was called back into the meeting room and informed that A&A was the only broker that had presented a non-binding indication and therefore had been selected to manage one of the largest private railroad networks in Brazil.

I could hardly believe it. Despite our lack of experience, our persistence paid off. The lesson here is clear: be persistent, never give up, and fight to the end — you might just be rewarded.

The Privatization Department was a huge success. For years, we eagerly followed the news, keeping an eye on which company would be privatized next so we could be the first to present our proposals.

We hired top engineers and insurance brokers, and our investments paid off as we secured many of the highways, railroads, ports, airports, and utility plants that were privatized. Once the main wave of privatizations ended, we renamed the Privatization Department as the Infrastructure Department, which became one of the most profitable divisions within A&A and Aon.

Another fascinating project I worked on was winning the bid to handle a large automotive assembly plant in Brazil. The fixed assets of any automotive plant are enormous, and the P&C (Property & Casualty) premiums are equally substantial. Securing this prestigious account was a significant achievement.

Winning the automotive plant account also brought in all the affiliated companies, including the captive bank, which financed the cars produced by the manufacturer. While the bank business wasn't as "exciting" as the industrial side, I volunteered to handle the bank's insurance needs.

After reviewing the insurance revenues generated by the incumbent broker, I believed we could do better. I convinced the bank president to provide us with the Broker of Record Letter (BORL), promising to develop a business plan that would surpass the existing insurance revenues.

All cars financed by the bank were required to be insured until the last installment was paid. Customers had the option to buy their own insurance and provide proof to the bank, or they could purchase the bank's auto insurance product. The existing product was expensive and required extensive paperwork. We needed to offer a more affordable option with less bureaucracy and faster policy issuance. We introduced the American F&I (Finance & Insurance) process to Brazil and set up a dedicated telemarketing team with a toll-free number to handle customer inquiries.

Our business plan aimed to close 6,000 auto insurance policies in the first year to meet our revenue targets and cover expenses. In our first month, we closed 6,000 policies. I initially thought it was beginner's luck, but the following month we closed 8,000 policies. My CEO became increasingly concerned because, until then, we had exclusively served about 1,000 large corporate clients. In just two months, our clientele had grown to 15,000, expanding from corporate clients to personal line clients. By the end of three years, we had closed approximately 360,000 auto insurance policies, successfully implementing the first F&I program in Brazil. This success prompted us to explore the Affinity market within our organization.

Golden rule # 10
Remove fear from your mind

Fear is a natural response to uncertainty, but in the world of business, it is often the single most significant barrier to innovation and success. The most successful entrepreneurs and managers understand that fear must be confronted and overcome, not just managed. It's about fostering a mindset that embraces creativity, courage, and a willingness to take calculated risks. These elements are essential for breaking new ground and achieving remarkable success. My journey in the insurance industry, particularly the development of the Financial Lines Department, is a testament to the power of removing fear from decision-making.

The challenge of surety bonding

At the turn of the century, our Surety-Bonding department was a modest operation. With just two employees, the department faced a significant challenge: the non-renewable nature of surety bonds. Unlike other insurance products that renew annually, surety bonds were tied to specific phases of construction. Once a phase was completed, the bond expired, and the department had to start from scratch each year. This lack of recurring revenue posed a severe obstacle to growth.

The situation demanded a creative solution, but creativity often requires stepping into the unknown, where fear can easily take hold. However, instead of succumbing to the fear of failure or the uncertainty of trying something new, I chose to confront the problem head-on.

Rebranding and expanding: a leap of faith

To rejuvenate the Surety-Bonding Department, I proposed a bold idea: rebrand it as the Financial Lines Department and introduce a new line of insurance that could generate more consistent revenue. Drawing on my experiences in the United States, I identified Directors and Officers (D&O) Insurance as a promising addition. This type of insurance, which protects corporate executives from personal losses due to legal actions taken against them, was gaining popularity in more developed markets. I believed it had strong potential in Brazil as well.

However, the first year was nothing short of a disaster. Despite our best efforts, we didn't close a single D&O policy. It would have been easy to let fear and doubt creep in, to abandon the new strategy and retreat to more familiar territory. But I knew that true innovation often involves setbacks and that these early failures were simply part of the process.

Overcoming setbacks: persistence and problem-solving

Determined to understand why our initial efforts had failed, I took a deeper dive into the situation. What I discovered was both enlightening and frustrating: most of our multinational clients in Brazil were already covered under master programs in the US and Europe. These programs were not only comprehensive but also illegal under Brazil's non-admitted insurance regulations. The problem was not our product, but our approach.

Rather than allowing this discovery to derail our efforts, we pivoted. I engaged one of the most prestigious legal firms in Brazil to draft a comprehensive legal opinion. This document clearly outlined the regulatory requirements for D&O insurance in Brazil, emphasizing that coverage had to be contracted locally to comply with the law. We distributed this information to our 500 offices worldwide, educating our clients on the necessity of local compliance.

This strategic pivot turned the tide. In the following years, we issued 450 D&O policies, effectively doubling the revenues of our newly formed Financial Lines Department. This success was not just about the financial gains; it was a validation of the importance of persistence, problem-solving, and the refusal to let fear dictate our actions.

The power of vision: expanding the portfolio

The success of the D&O policies provided the stability that our Surety-Bonding Department desperately needed. However, I recognized that two lines of insurance — surety bonds and D&O — were not sufficient to sustain long-term growth. In 2001, I decided to introduce Trade Credit Insurance to our portfolio. This decision was driven by a combination of foresight and a willingness to take a calculated risk.

At the time, the trade credit insurance market in Brazil was virtually non-existent, with only one insurer operating in the country. Many would have seen this as a deterrent, but I saw it as an opportunity. Based on my international experiences, I believed that major trade credit insurers would soon enter the Brazilian market, and I wanted our firm to be ready when they did.

This was a risky move. Expanding into a new market segment with limited existing infrastructure could have backfired. But I trusted my instincts and the experience I had gained from similar markets abroad. By 2005, my predictions proved accurate. The main players in the trade credit insurance market had established operations in Brazil, and by then, we were the only broker in the country with a dedicated team for trade credit insurance. We commanded nearly 80% of the market, a remarkable achievement that stemmed from the courage to take a risk when others hesitated.

The entrepreneurial leap: facing the unknown

By 2007, I was 47 years old, and according to the career plan I had outlined earlier in my life, it was time to consider the next phase of my journey. The success of our Financial Lines Department had attracted significant attention, leading to several job offers, including a partnership in a British reinsurance brokerage firm. However, I felt the pull to do something more radical — something that would allow me to fully embrace the entrepreneurial spirit that had driven my career thus far.

Leaving the security of a stable job with guaranteed salary and benefits to start my own company was a daunting prospect. The fear of the unknown loomed large, as it does for anyone contemplating such a significant life change. But I knew that if I was to achieve something truly meaningful, I had to move beyond that fear.

I made the decision to establish CredRisk Seguros, the first specialized trade credit insurance brokerage house in Brazil. This was not a decision made lightly; it was a calculated risk, backed by a decade-long business plan focused on profitability rather than size. My vision was clear: to build a niche firm that would allow me to make a comfortable income while enjoying the remaining years of my professional career.

In February 2007, I handed in my resignation letter at Aon Risk Services and took the plunge into entrepreneurship. The fear was there, but I refused to let it hold me back. And as with every major decision in my career, the rewards of stepping into the unknown proved to be deeply gratifying.

Embracing courage over fear

The story of my journey — from rebranding the Surety-Bonding Department to launching CredRisk Seguros — is a testament to the power of removing fear from the equation. Every significant achievement in my career has been the result of facing fear head-on, making bold decisions, and refusing to let setbacks define the outcome.

Fear, when left unchecked, can paralyze action and stifle innovation. But when confronted and managed, it can become a powerful motivator, driving us to take the risks necessary for success. So, remove fear from your mind, and let your actions be guided by the possibilities, not the limitations.

Chapter Three

Golden rule # 3
You can't change the world, but you can change yourself

This golden rule is not merely a motivational quote; it's a practical guide to overcoming the internal barriers that often prevent people from realizing their dreams. The world around us is complex and ever-changing, and while we may not have the power to change these external factors, we do have the ability to change ourselves — our mindset, our approach, and our resilience. This internal transformation is the first step toward building something from nothing, toward taking that leap of faith required to start a business.

When I decided to establish a specialized trade credit insurance brokerage in Brazil, it was not an easy decision. I was stepping away from the security of a well-established career and into a space that had never been explored before in the Brazilian market. The idea of a mono-line, specialized trade credit insurance brokerage was unheard of. It was a significant professional and financial risk, and the fear of the unknown was very real. But I knew that to succeed, I needed to conquer that fear and focus on what I could control — my own actions and decisions.

Golden rule # 11 "Genius is 1% inspiration and 99% perspiration" – Thomas Edison

The idea of establishing a mono-line, specialized trade credit insurance brokerage house came to me in a moment of inspiration. It was a Sunday morning, and my wife and I were walking along an exotic beach in Brazil. The idea struck me like a bolt of lightning — a fleeting thought that quickly took root in my mind. But as Thomas Edison so wisely said, "Genius is 1% inspiration and 99% perspiration". That brief moment of inspiration was just the beginning; what followed was months of hard work, planning, and preparation.

Over the following months, I meticulously prepared a comprehensive 10-year business plan and action plan that would guide me through the next decade. This plan was my roadmap, outlining every step I needed to take to turn that fleeting thought into a reality. The "perspiration" part of Edison's equation involved countless hours of research, strategy sessions, and financial planning. It was not glamorous work, but it was necessary to build a solid foundation for the company.

The great inventor's observation about genius being mostly hard work couldn't be more accurate. The initial idea, while important, was just a small part of the overall journey. The real challenge — and ultimately, the real reward — came from the sustained effort required to bring that idea to fruition. Over the next fifteen years, through dedication, persistence, and a relentless focus on execution, I was able to build the best and largest trade credit insurance brokerage house in Brazil.

The path to success: from inspiration to reality

My initial goal wasn't to create the largest trade credit insurance brokerage in Brazil, but rather the most profitable. Profitability was always the primary focus. I knew that in order to survive and thrive in the competitive insurance market, the company needed to be financially sound and consistently profitable.

However, as we executed our strategy and built our reputation, a "collateral effect" of our success was becoming the largest in the market.

Venture capitalists and business experts often emphasize the importance of focusing on profitability over sheer size, and this approach proved to be particularly effective in our case. By concentrating on profitability, we were able to reinvest in the business, attract top talent, and provide exceptional service to our clients. These factors combined to fuel our growth, eventually leading us to become the market leader.

The decision to establish CredRisk Seguros in June 2007 was a turning point in my career. It was a bold move into uncharted territory, with no guarantees of success. When we issued our first policy in October of that same year, it was a moment of both relief and validation. Our first client was a Brazilian bank, which, I'm proud to say, remains one of our most important clients 17 years later. This long-term relationship is a testament to the quality of our service and the trust we have built over the years.

If you can't measure it, you can't manage it

From day one at CredRisk Seguros, I was focused on management reports and ensuring we had the best backend and frontend software available in the Brazilian market. This focus on measurement and data-driven decision-making was critical to our success. The ability to measure performance in real time allows for more effective management, quicker adjustments, and better strategic planning.

The softwares we implemented in 2007 were state-of-the-art, and I'm proud to say that an updated version of these softwares are the same ones in use by MDS today. This continuity speaks to the quality and effectiveness of the systems we put in place. By investing in top-tier technology, we were able to streamline our operations, improve client service, and maintain a competitive edge in the market.

One of the key lessons I learned early in my career is encapsulated in the saying, "If you can't measure it, you can't manage it." This principle is especially true in the insurance brokerage business, where profitability depends on precise management of revenues, costs, and risks. Having all the information you need at your fingertips, in real time, is crucial for making informed decisions and steering the company in the right direction.

The importance of profitability: a financial philosophy

The Profit & Loss (P&L) statement is one of the most important accounting reports because it allows you to monitor the profitability of your company. Since 1978, my philosophy has always been to focus on profitability rather than just revenue. While gross and net revenues are important, the real focus should be on the bottom line — net operating income before tax, or the company's profitability.

Profitability is the ultimate measure of a company's success. It's not enough to bring in revenue; what matters is how much of that revenue you can retain as profit. This focus on the bottom line guided every decision I made, from staffing to pricing to investment in technology. By maintaining a disciplined approach to profitability, we were able to build a financially robust company that could weather the ups and downs of the market.

My standard approach was that the brokerage house needed to produce a net operating income of 25% to 35% per year. This profit margin is well above what financial markets offer in interest rates on investments in Brazil, making it more sensible to invest in the brokerage company rather than in the financial markets. This philosophy not only ensured the company's financial health but also allowed us to reinvest in growth and innovation.

Controlling costs: the key to sustainable profitability

To achieve this level of profitability, controlling costs and expenses is essential. Brokerage houses have two main categories of costs and expenses. The first and most significant is "staff costs." In an efficient brokerage, staff costs should not exceed 45% to 50% of net revenues. Staff costs include salaries, benefits, bonuses, and labor taxes. Managing these costs effectively requires a balance between attracting and retaining top talent and maintaining a lean, efficient operation.

The second category is broadly known as "other costs," which should not exceed 20% to 25% of net revenues. These include office expenses like rent and utilities, marketing, accounting, technology, legal fees, indirect taxes, and other miscellaneous expenses. While these costs are necessary for the day-to-day operation of the business, keeping them in check is crucial for maintaining healthy profit margins.

Monitoring this revenue and cost structure monthly is key to maintaining profitability between 25% and 35%. Regular reviews of financial performance allow for timely adjustments and ensure that the company stays on track to meet its financial goals. This disciplined approach to cost management has been a cornerstone of our success at CredRisk Seguros and is a practice I recommend to any business manager seeking to build a profitable enterprise.

As previously discussed, a brokerage business in which staff costs exceed 50% of net revenues is often seen as operating inefficiently. Such a high ratio suggests that personnel expenses are disproportionately large relative to the income generated.

This typically points to an inflated headcount or insufficient revenue per employee — both of which threaten the sustainability of the business model. On the other hand, if total staff costs account for only 20% of net revenues, that too can be a red flag. Why?

First, it may indicate that employees are underpaid, which can lead to dissatisfaction, low morale, and disengagement. An unhappy team is unlikely to deliver the exceptional service that clients expect — and deserve. Second, it may signal that the business is understaffed, which can compromise service quality. Inadequate staffing can slow response times, diminish client satisfaction, and ultimately damage the firm's reputation.

To manage these risks effectively, it's essential to rely on accurate financial reporting and well-defined Key Performance Indicators (KPIs). These tools provide the insights necessary to evaluate and improve operational efficiency. As the saying goes, "If you can't measure it, you can't manage it." By establishing clear metrics and monitoring them regularly, you'll be better equipped to manage your operations and will distinguish your company from the competition.

Expenses should chase revenues, not the other way around

The principle that "Expenses should chase revenues, not the other way around" is a cornerstone of sound financial management, especially in industries where revenue streams can be unpredictable, such as insurance brokerage. This philosophy is not just about controlling costs; it's about ensuring the sustainability and profitability of your business in the long term.

The role of corporate governance

Corporate governance refers to the system of rules, practices, and processes by which a company is directed and controlled. It involves balancing the interests of a company's many stakeholders, including shareholders, management, customers, suppliers, financiers, government, and the community.

Good corporate governance is not just about compliance with laws and regulations; it is a mindset that should be ingrained in all managers and leaders within the organization. It involves creating a culture of transparency, accountability, and ethical behavior that permeates every level of the company. When corporate governance is taken seriously, it can help prevent many of the issues that lead to tax and labor liabilities in the first place.

For example, by fostering a culture of transparency, a company can ensure that all financial transactions are properly recorded and reported, reducing the risk of tax evasion or fraud. Similarly, by promoting ethical behavior and fair treatment of employees, a company can minimize the likelihood of labor disputes and the resulting liabilities.

Corporate governance also involves the implementation of internal controls and risk management practices that help identify potential liabilities before they become problematic. This includes regular audits, both internal and external, to ensure compliance with all legal and regulatory requirements, as well as the continuous monitoring of key performance indicators that could signal emerging risks.

Building a legacy through discipline and innovation

The journey of establishing and growing CredRisk Seguros has been one of the most rewarding experiences of my professional life. It has taught me the importance of discipline, innovation, and a relentless focus on profitability. By following the golden rules, I was able to build a company that not only survived in a competitive market but thrived.

As I reflect on the past fifteen years, I see the wisdom in these principles and how they have shaped both my business and personal life. They are not just guidelines for success in business; they are philosophies that can be applied to any endeavor in life. Whether you are starting a new company, embarking on a personal project, or simply trying to improve yourself, these golden rules can provide the foundation for lasting success.

In the end, the legacy of CredRisk Seguros is not just in the numbers or the market share, but in the lessons learned and the principles upheld. It's about building something that stands the test of time, something that not only changes the industry but also changes you as a person. And that, perhaps, is the greatest achievement of all.

Golden rule # 12
Take risks

Taking risks is an inherent part of entrepreneurship and a critical factor in achieving success. Many aspiring entrepreneurs fall into the trap of waiting for the perfect moment or ideal conditions before taking the plunge into starting their own business. They believe that if they can just time it right, everything will align perfectly, and their venture will be an instant success. However, the reality is far different — there is rarely, if ever, a perfect moment to start a business. The key to success lies in the willingness to take risks, even when the timing seems less than ideal.

The fallacy of the perfect moment

The idea that there is a "perfect" time to start a business or a new project is a comforting illusion, but it's also a dangerous one. This mindset can lead to endless procrastination, with potential entrepreneurs constantly waiting for conditions to improve, for the economy to stabilize, or for personal circumstances to become more favorable. While it's natural to want to mitigate risk, waiting for perfection often results in missed opportunities. The truth is, no matter how carefully you plan, there will always be uncertainties and challenges that you cannot predict or control.

In my own experience, when Luiz Inácio Lula da Silva won the Brazilian presidential election, in 2002, and was reelected four years later, many people were anxious about the future of the country. The prevailing sentiment was one of uncertainty and concern, leading many to consider leaving Brazil rather than starting new ventures. Despite this atmosphere of caution, I decided to take a risk and establish my company. Some years later, in 2008, the world was hit by the worst credit crisis since 1929. On the surface, it seemed like I couldn't have chosen a worse time to launch a mono-line trade credit insurance brokerage. But as it turned out, this challenging period offered unique opportunities that I could never have anticipated.

Turning adversity into opportunity

The global economic crisis of 2008 had a profound impact on businesses around the world, and Brazil was no exception. As the crisis unfolded, trade credit insurers in Brazil began withdrawing credit limits from their clients, which led to widespread dissatisfaction among large corporate clients. This dissatisfaction created a demand for alternatives, and because I had taken the risk of starting my business during this turbulent time, I was in a prime position to capitalize on this opportunity.

While many established players in the market struggled to adapt to the new economic reality, my company was agile and responsive. We quickly gained several large corporate clients who were looking for alternatives to the "alpha brokers" who had dominated the market. By taking a risk and entering the market at a time when others were retreating, we were able to carve out a niche and establish ourselves as a viable and competitive player in the industry.

The lesson here is clear: if you wait for the perfect time to start a new company or a new project, you may never start at all. The conditions that seem unfavorable today could be the very factors that create opportunities for success tomorrow. Taking risks doesn't mean acting recklessly; it means being willing to move forward even when the path ahead is uncertain.

Continuous learning and adaptation

In addition to taking risks and building financial reserves, continuous learning is essential for long-term success. Earlier in this book, I emphasized the importance of formal education and training, particularly in the early stages of your career. However, learning should not stop once you've established yourself in your field. The business world is constantly evolving, and staying informed about new developments, trends, and best practices is crucial.

Even as we age and our priorities shift, there are still many ways to continue learning. Reading books, attending seminars, and listening to TED Talks are all excellent ways to keep your mind sharp and stay ahead of the curve. I'm a firm believer in the adage that "Leaders are Readers." Over the past twenty years, I've read about a hundred books, each one offering new insights and perspectives that have informed my approach to business and leadership.

One book that I highly recommend to all entrepreneurs and executives is Jim Rohn's "The Seasons of Life." This classic work offers timeless wisdom on the natural cycles of life and business, teaching us to prepare for the inevitable ups and downs that come with the territory. Understanding these cycles and adapting to them is a crucial part of managing risk and achieving long-term success.

My top three book recommendations

The Seasons of Life
by Jim Rohn

Who Moved My Cheese?
by Spencer Johnson

Think and Grow Rich
by Napoleon Hill

Embrace risk as a pathway to success

Taking risks is not just an option in business; it's a necessity. The fear of failure or the desire for perfect timing can paralyze even the most talented individuals, preventing them from realizing their potential. But those who are willing to take calculated risks, to venture into the unknown, and to embrace uncertainty are the ones who ultimately achieve the greatest success.

Remember, there will never be a perfect time to start a new company or a new project. Economic conditions, market dynamics, and personal circumstances will always present challenges. But by building financial reserves, continuing to learn and adapt, and most importantly, taking risks when others hesitate, you can turn these challenges into opportunities. The path to success is rarely smooth, but it's the willingness to take risks that often makes the difference between failure and greatness. In the end, risk-taking is about more than just financial gain; it's about growth, learning, and the pursuit of something greater. It's about pushing beyond your comfort zone and daring to achieve what others might consider impossible. So, take that leap, embrace the uncertainty, and remember that the greatest rewards often come from the greatest risks.

Golden rule # 13 Be a reference in your field of business

Becoming a recognized expert in your field is not just a goal — it's a strategic imperative that can significantly enhance your career and the success of your business. Establishing yourself as a reference point within your industry brings credibility, attracts opportunities, and differentiates you from your competitors. However, this level of recognition doesn't come overnight; it requires deliberate effort, ongoing education, and active participation in relevant professional communities.

Active participation in professional communities

One of the most effective ways to establish yourself as an expert in your field is through active participation in professional communities and industry organizations. Throughout my career, I made it a priority to engage with as many chambers of commerce as possible, particularly those that were relevant to my line of business. While it's impractical to join every chamber, carefully selecting a few that align with your industry can provide invaluable networking opportunities and help you build lasting relationships.

In Brazil, for example, I ensured that we were members of the British, American, Swedish, and Portuguese Chambers of Commerce. Each of these organizations offered unique opportunities to connect with business managers, share insights, and stay informed about industry trends. These interactions not only broadened my professional network but also enhanced my understanding of different market dynamics, which in turn benefited my business.

Beyond chambers of commerce, I joined the Brazilian Institute of Financial Executives (Instituto Brasileiro de Executivos de Finanças - IBEF). This organization was particularly important because financial managers and directors often play a crucial role as "economic buyers" in my sales process. By being part of IBEF, I could directly engage with these key decision-makers, understand their concerns, and position my services as solutions to their problems.

Industry representation and leadership

In addition to participating in professional communities, taking on leadership roles within industry organizations can further solidify your reputation as an expert. For instance, I became a member of the São Paulo Brokers Union (SINCOR-SP), which represents a significant portion of the broker community in Brazil, with approximately 70,000 members. Being involved in such a large and influential organization provided me with a platform to advocate for the interests of my peers and to contribute to the development of industry standards.

My involvement with SINCOR-SP led to an invitation to join the Credit & Surety Committee, where I could represent the members' interests within both the business and governmental communities. This role not only allowed me to influence policy and practice within the industry but also positioned me as a trusted voice among my colleagues and clients. By taking on such responsibilities, you demonstrate your commitment to the advancement of your field, which enhances your credibility and visibility.

Academic contributions and thought leadership

Another powerful way to establish yourself as a reference in your field is by contributing to the academic and intellectual discourse surrounding your industry. In 2017, I was honored to be elected as an Insurance Academic by the Academia Nacional de Seguros e Previdência (ANSP), the National Academy for Insurance and Pensions. This recognition was a testament to my expertise and my contributions to the field of insurance.

But my commitment to advancing knowledge didn't stop there. In 2019, I authored my first book, "Introduction to Credit Insurance in Brazil." This was a significant achievement, particularly because the last book on this subject in Portuguese had been written 51 years earlier, in 1968. By filling this gap in the literature, I provided a valuable resource for both students and professionals, further cementing my status as a thought leader in the industry.

Writing a book or contributing articles to industry publications is an excellent way to share your expertise and influence the direction of your field. It not only showcases your knowledge but also ensures that your ideas and insights reach a wider audience, thereby increasing your impact.

Building and maintaining a strong team

While individual recognition is important, the success of any business ultimately depends on the strength and dedication of its team. As our business grew, the need to hire new employees became apparent. I have always taken the hiring process very seriously, applying a methodical approach to selecting the best candidates. This meticulousness sometimes frustrated my executives, as it often took several months to find the right person. However, I firmly believe that it is better to be thorough in the hiring process than to make a hasty decision that could lead to problems down the road.

Each candidate typically went through four or five interviews with my staff before I would interview them personally. This rigorous process ensured that we only hired individuals who not only had the necessary skills and experience but also aligned with our company's values and culture. The result was a highly successful, people-driven business where employees felt valued and were motivated to contribute to our collective success.

Investing in your team doesn't end with hiring; retaining top talent is equally important. We have always allocated significant resources to ensure our employees are well compensated, receive ongoing training, and feel like an integral part of the company. At CredRisk Seguros, we fostered a family-like environment where everyone is treated with respect and consideration. This approach has led to high employee retention rates and a strong, cohesive team that drives our business forward.

The importance of intellectual and technological expertise

In today's fast-paced business environment, it's crucial to invest not only in your intellectual growth but also in technological advancements. Staying at the forefront of technological developments allows you to offer innovative solutions to your clients and maintain a competitive edge. Throughout my career, I have made it a point to stay informed about the latest technological trends and to implement them within our business operations.

Intellectual expertise is equally important. Continuously expanding your knowledge, whether through formal education, attending conferences, or self-study, is essential to staying relevant in your field. As I've emphasized before, leaders are readers. Keeping up with industry literature, reading widely, and staying curious are all part of what it takes to remain a reference in your field.

The journey to becoming a reference

Becoming a reference in your field of business is a journey that requires dedication, continuous learning, and active participation in your industry. It's about more than just being good at what you do — it's about being recognized by your peers, clients, and the broader community as someone who sets the standard for excellence.

By engaging in professional communities, taking on leadership roles, contributing to academic discourse, building a strong team, and staying at the forefront of technological and intellectual advancements, you can position yourself as a true expert in your field. This not only differentiates you from the competition but also opens up new opportunities for growth, collaboration, and success.

In the end, the effort you put into becoming a reference in your field will pay off in countless ways, both professionally and personally. It will allow you to make a lasting impact on your industry, inspire others, and achieve the kind of success that comes from being recognized as a leader in your domain.

Golden rule # 14
Surround yourself with people better than you

The success of any venture is rarely the result of a single individual's efforts. More often, it is the collective strength of a team — composed of people who bring diverse skills, experiences, and perspectives — that drives a company to greatness. As the founder and leader of CredRisk Seguros, I can attest that our achievements were built on the foundation of a strong, capable team. This is why the fourteenth golden rule in my book is to surround yourself with people who are better than you.

The power of a strong team

When I reflect on the success of CredRisk Seguros, I am acutely aware that it was the result of our "family" of superb collaborators. From the cleaning staff who maintained a welcoming and organized environment, to the account executives who tirelessly served our clients, to my partner who shared in the vision and challenges of growing the business — each person played a critical role in our success. The collective dedication, talent, and commitment of our team enabled us to rise to the position of the leading trade credit insurance brokerage house in Brazil.

It's important to recognize that no manager can do it all. The most successful managers are those who understand their own limitations and intentionally build teams that complement their weaknesses and enhance their strengths. By surrounding yourself with people who are better than you in various areas, you create a dynamic environment where innovation flourishes, and challenges are met with effective solutions. This approach not only elevates the performance of the team but also drives the entire organization forward.

The role of external consultants

In addition to building a strong internal team, another key to success is enlisting the help of excellent, trusted external advisors. While your internal team handles the day-to-day operations and execution, external consultants bring specialized expertise and an outsider's perspective that is invaluable, especially in times of crisis.

Throughout my years running CredRisk Seguros, I always sought out the best professionals I could afford to guide us in areas where we needed external support. This included lawyers who provided critical legal guidance, tax advisors who helped us navigate the complexities of Brazil's tax system, accountants who ensured our financial health, marketing experts who enhanced our brand presence, and human resource consultants who helped us attract and retain top talent.

The importance of having these trusted advisors cannot be overstated. In business, crises are inevitable. Whether it's an economic downturn, a legal challenge, or a sudden shift in the market, there will be moments when your company faces significant obstacles. It is during these times that the value of having a strong network of external consultants becomes most apparent. Trying to find good professionals in the midst of a crisis is a recipe for disaster.

It's far better to establish these relationships early, so you can rely on their expertise when you need it most.

A culture of continuous improvement

Surrounding yourself with people who are better than you also fosters a culture of continuous improvement within your organization. When you bring in team members and consultants who excel in their fields, it sets a high standard for everyone. It encourages a mindset where learning and development are prioritized, and where individuals are motivated to constantly improve their skills and knowledge.

As a leader, this means being humble enough to recognize that you don't have all the answers and being open to the insights and suggestions of others. It means creating an environment where collaboration is valued, and where the best ideas — no matter where they come from — are given the space to flourish. This approach not only enhances the capabilities of your team but also drives innovation and success in your business.

The legacy of a great team

In the end, the legacy of a successful business is not just in its financial performance or market position, but in the strength and cohesion of its team. The relationships you build with your employees, partners, and external consultants are what sustain the business through both the good and the bad. When you surround yourself with people who are better than you, you create a foundation that can withstand challenges and continue to grow and evolve over time.

At CredRisk Seguros, I am proud of the team we built and the culture we fostered. Our employees were not just workers; they were part of a family, and they were treated as such. This sense of belonging and shared purpose was a significant factor in our long-term success. It's a reminder that the people you choose to surround yourself with are not just contributors to your business — they are the lifeblood of it.

I would like to share with you one of our successful stories regarding the acquisition of a new account involving our CredRisk team.

In 2014 I visited a large supplier in the agro sector. Listening to the prospect, it came over to me loud and clear that the company was using a very experienced and competent insurance broker. The risk manager's main concern was that the insurance broker was a "one-man show" and if anything happened to that individual they would be in deep trouble. I took note of all the details of the meeting and asked the risk manager if I could return in a week's time with our proposal to take over the account.

The following week I marched into the meeting room with ten well-dressed and prepared professionals to pitch our proposal to the risk manager. The risk manager was puzzled to see so many executives in one meeting. I told him that from this day forward he would have a dedicated team of ten people on his account.

Each member of the team stood up and made his specific presentation, covering all aspects of the account from helping to approve credit limits to the liquidation of future claims. For each specific area we had a competent professional to assist the client. We left that meeting with the Broker of Record Letter.

This was a classic example that teamwork wins accounts.

Summing up, golden rule #14 is about recognizing that true leadership is not about being the smartest person in the room; it's about building a team of people who bring diverse strengths and perspectives that complement your own. By surrounding yourself with individuals who are better than you — both within your organization and through external partnerships — you set the stage for success. You create an environment where challenges are met with confidence, where innovation thrives, and where your business can achieve its full potential.

So, as you build your team and seek out advisors, remember to look for those who can bring something more to the table — whether it's deeper expertise, fresh ideas, or a different perspective. In doing so, you'll not only elevate your business but also create a legacy of excellence that will endure long after you've moved on to new challenges.

Golden rule # 15
Keep improving best practices

In the fast-paced and competitive world of business, maintaining a high standard of professionalism is not just about meeting expectations — it's about exceeding them consistently. This is where the principle of Best Practices comes into play. Best Practices are the methods or techniques that have consistently shown superior results and are therefore used as benchmarks. However, what distinguishes truly successful businesses is their commitment to continuously improving these practices.

The power of professionalism

The foundation of any successful business lies in its professionalism. This encompasses everything from punctuality and the quality of presentations to maintaining a polished appearance and ensuring timely communication. While these may seem like small details, they collectively shape the perception of your business in the eyes of clients, partners, and competitors. They are the building blocks of trust and credibility.

Being punctual, for instance, is more than just a matter of showing respect for other people's time; it reflects your reliability and discipline. When you deliver a presentation that is not only well-prepared but also finely tuned to the needs and expectations of your audience, it demonstrates your expertise and commitment to excellence. Maintaining a professional appearance reinforces your brand and shows that you take your role seriously. Promptly returning phone calls and responding to emails convey your responsiveness and dedication to client service.

These seemingly minor actions contribute significantly to how your business is perceived. They create a consistent experience for your clients, where they know they can rely on you to deliver not just satisfactory results but exceptional ones. This level of professionalism sets the stage for long-term success, fostering loyalty and encouraging repeat business.

The continuous improvement mindset

However, professionalism alone is not enough. To truly excel, you must adopt a mindset of continuous improvement. This means recognizing that no matter how well you are doing today, there is always room for enhancement. Alastair's advice that "successful brokers must be lazy and intelligent" encapsulates this idea. It's about working smarter, not harder, by refining your processes and focusing on what truly adds value.

Continuous improvement is not about making sweeping changes or reinventing your business model every day. Instead, it's about making incremental, consistent enhancements to your daily operations. For example, consider your presentations. Rather than settling for a format that works, look for ways to make them even more engaging — perhaps by incorporating more visual elements, simplifying complex information, or tailoring your message more closely to your audience's needs.

Similarly, fine-tuning your processes — whether in client onboarding, project management, or service delivery — can lead to significant gains in efficiency and effectiveness over time. By regularly reviewing and refining these processes, you can eliminate unnecessary steps, reduce errors, and ensure that your business operations are as smooth and streamlined as possible.

Transforming good into great

The real magic of continuous improvement lies in its cumulative effect. When you make small, consistent improvements day after day, these enhancements compound over time, transforming a good company into a great one. This is the essence of the Japanese concept of "Kaizen," which emphasizes continuous improvement in all aspects of life, including business. By focusing on gradual, ongoing development, you not only keep your business competitive but also create a culture of excellence that permeates every level of your organization.

Moreover, this commitment to improvement helps you stay ahead of the curve. In a rapidly changing business environment, those who rest on their laurels are quickly left behind. By continuously refining your Best Practices, you ensure that your business is always evolving, adapting to new challenges, and seizing new opportunities. This proactive approach keeps your clients satisfied, as they can see the tangible benefits of your dedication to excellence.

The client-centric approach

At the heart of improving Best Practices is the desire to better serve your clients. After all, a business's success is ultimately determined by how well it meets its clients' needs. By continuously enhancing your service capabilities, you demonstrate a commitment to your clients' success, which in turn fosters loyalty and long-term relationships.

For example, by refining your communication processes — ensuring that emails are answered promptly, calls are returned quickly, and client queries are addressed thoroughly — you build a reputation for being responsive and dependable. When clients know they can count on you to be there when they need you, they are more likely to trust you with their business and recommend your services to others.

Similarly, by improving the quality of your presentations and reports, you make it easier for clients to understand complex information and make informed decisions. This not only enhances their experience but also positions you as a valuable partner in their success.

The path to excellence

Golden rule #15 emphasizes that the journey to excellence is never-ending. It's about continually raising the bar for yourself and your business, not by making dramatic changes, but by consistently refining and improving your Best Practices. This commitment to continuous improvement is what separates the good from the great and ensures that your business remains competitive and relevant in a constantly evolving marketplace.

By focusing on professionalism, adopting a mindset of continuous improvement, and always striving to better serve your clients, you lay the groundwork for long-term success. Remember, it's the small, everyday improvements that, over time, create a profound impact on your business. So, keep refining, keep improving, and keep pushing the boundaries of what's possible. This is how you turn a good company into a great one and how you build a legacy of excellence that stands the test of time.

Golden rule # 16
Be the "go-to" person in your organization

In any organization, there are always those individuals who stand out — not necessarily because they hold the highest positions, but because they are the ones everyone turns to when something important needs to be done. These are the "go-to" people, the ones who consistently deliver results, solve problems, and drive projects to successful completion. Becoming the "go-to" person in your organization is one of the most effective ways to accelerate your career, build your reputation, and make a lasting impact.

The power of being the "go-to" person

Being the "go-to" person means that others trust you to handle critical tasks and responsibilities. This trust is not given lightly; it is earned through consistent performance, reliability, and the ability to deliver under pressure. When you establish yourself as the person who can be relied upon in any situation, you become invaluable to your organization. This value is not only recognized by your peers but also by your superiors, who will likely consider you for promotions, important assignments, and leadership roles.

At CredRisk Seguros, I was fortunate to have several reliable “go-to” executives who made my life easier and our company even stronger. These individuals were not just technically proficient — they were also proactive, resourceful, and committed to the success of the organization. Their ability to take ownership of tasks and see them through to completion was a key factor in our company’s growth and success.

How to become the “go-to” person? To become the “go-to” person in your organization, you need to cultivate a few key traits and behaviors:

Reliability: The foundation of being a “go-to” person is reliability. You must be someone who consistently delivers on promises and meets deadlines. This means managing your time effectively, prioritizing tasks, and being organized. When others know they can count on you, they will naturally turn to you when they need something done.

Proactivity: Don’t wait for tasks to be assigned to you — seek them out. Look for areas where you can contribute, identify problems before they escalate, and offer solutions. Proactive individuals are often the first to be noticed and appreciated in any organization because they demonstrate initiative and a strong work ethic.

Problem-Solving: Being the "go-to" person often involves tackling difficult problems. Develop your problem-solving skills by staying calm under pressure, thinking critically, and approaching challenges with a solutions-oriented mindset. When you are known as someone who can handle complex situations, your value to the organization increases exponentially.

Expertise: Build deep expertise in your area of responsibility. Whether it's through formal education, on-the-job experience, or continuous learning, strive to become the most knowledgeable person in your field. When others recognize your expertise, they will naturally seek your input and guidance.

Communication: Effective communication is crucial. As the "go-to" person, you will often need to coordinate with different teams, explain your ideas clearly, and ensure that everyone is on the same page. Good communication fosters collaboration and helps you build strong relationships across the organization.

Dependability in Crisis: Crises are inevitable in any business. How you handle these moments can define your career. Being the "go-to" person means stepping up when things go wrong, providing leadership, and helping to navigate the organization through tough times. Your ability to remain composed and decisive during a crisis will cement your reputation as a key player.

The benefits of being the "go-to" person

The benefits of establishing yourself as the "go-to" person extend far beyond the immediate recognition you receive. It can lead to faster career progression, as decision-makers in the organization will see you as someone who is capable of taking on more responsibility. This can result in promotions, raises, and the opportunity to work on high-profile projects that further your professional development.

Additionally, being the "go-to" person enhances your job security. In times of organizational change, companies are less likely to part with employees who are seen as indispensable. Your reputation as a reliable and effective problem-solver makes you a critical asset to the organization, giving you a greater degree of job stability.

Moreover, the skills and experience you gain from being the "go-to" person are transferable. Whether you stay with your current company or move on to new opportunities, the reputation you build will follow you. Employers value candidates who have demonstrated the ability to take initiative and deliver results in previous roles.

Fostering a culture of "go-to" people

As a manager, it's important not only to be a "go-to" person yourself but also to cultivate this quality in your team. Encourage your team members to take ownership of their tasks, develop their problem-solving skills, and seek out opportunities to contribute. By fostering a culture where everyone strives to be a "go-to" person, you strengthen the overall capability of your organization and create a more resilient, agile workforce.

At CredRisk Seguros, the presence of multiple "go-to" executives was a significant factor in our success. It allowed us to distribute responsibility effectively, ensure that critical tasks were always in capable hands, and respond swiftly to challenges. This culture of reliability and excellence permeated every level of the organization, contributing to our strong performance and reputation in the market.

In a nutshell, golden rule #16 — Be the "go-to" person in your organization — is about more than just advancing your career; it's about making a meaningful impact within your company. By consistently delivering results, being proactive, and developing your expertise, you can establish yourself as an indispensable member of your team. This reputation not only benefits you but also strengthens your organization as a whole.

Remember, the path to becoming the "go-to" person is paved with dedication, hard work, and a commitment to excellence. It requires you to step up when others hesitate, take on challenges with confidence, and continuously seek ways to add value. In doing so, you will not only achieve personal success but also contribute to the success and growth of your organization.

I have a compelling real-world example of what it truly means to be the "go-to" person within an organization. Each year, we recruited a group of recent university graduates to join our company as trainees. Typically, we hired between five and ten individuals with degrees in areas such as insurance, business, economics, engineering, or law, and enrolled them in a comprehensive training program that rotated through the company's core departments.

However, by the end of the first year, on average, roughly half of the trainees would choose to leave. The demands of the job were simply too high relative to the compensation offered. Among those who stayed — the "survivors" — the pressure intensified. They were closely evaluated and given significant responsibilities. Over time, a small number stood out as the true "high potentials," and we began investing heavily in their professional development. One of these high-potential trainees eventually became the CEO of a 2,000 -plus employee organization — he was also in his mid-forties when he became the CEO. What set him apart? He had built a reputation throughout the organization as the "go-to" person—someone who could always be counted on to get things done, and to do them exceptionally well.

My advice to all young professionals is this: strive to become the "go-to" person in your organization. Take on as many projects as you can handle, and deliver outstanding results every time. By consistently proving your reliability, competence, and drive, you'll position yourself for advancement—whether that means rising to the top of your company or launching your own entrepreneurial journey.

Golden rule # 17
Find happiness

In the pursuit of a successful career, many people focus on external achievements — financial success, professional recognition, and career advancement. While these are important, they often overlook a critical element that underpins all long-term success: happiness. Happiness is not just a nice-to-have; it is essential to a successful and fulfilling career. Without it, even the most significant accomplishments can feel hollow and unsatisfying.

The role of happiness in success

Happiness plays a fundamental role in our ability to perform well as professionals and entrepreneurs. When we are happy, we are more motivated, more creative, and more resilient in the face of challenges. Happiness fuels our passion and drives us to excel in our endeavors. It gives us the energy and enthusiasm needed to push through difficult times and to keep moving forward even when the path is tough.

On the other hand, when we are unhappy, everything becomes more difficult. Our productivity decreases, our stress levels rise, and our overall sense of well-being suffers. It becomes harder to maintain the focus and determination needed to achieve our goals. This is why finding happiness is not just about personal fulfillment; it is also a strategic component of success.

The three pillars of happiness

Happiness, as I see it, is built on three basic elements: enjoyment, satisfaction, and meaningfulness. Each of these elements contributes to a well-rounded and lasting sense of happiness, and together they form the foundation for a successful and fulfilling career.

1. Enjoyment:

In a professional context, it is crucial to find work that you genuinely enjoy. This doesn't mean that every task will be pleasurable, but overall, you should derive a sense of enjoyment from your work. When you enjoy what you do, work feels less like a chore and more like a natural expression of your skills and interests. This enjoyment fuels your motivation and helps you maintain a positive attitude, even during challenging times. Enjoyment is the immediate pleasure and joy we derive from our daily activities. It's the feeling of being engaged and absorbed in what we're doing — whether it's working on a project, spending time with loved ones, or pursuing a hobby. It's about being present in the moment and finding satisfaction in the process, not just in the outcomes.

For me, it was a pleasure to go into the office every day. I would wake up every morning ready to face the challenges of the job. I genuinely enjoyed working with my coworkers — and even more so, with the many different clients I had the privilege to serve.

Insurance is insurance — but no two clients were ever the same. I worked across different sectors of the economy and in various regions of the country. What might seem like a repetitive and monotonous job turned out to be incredibly interesting and dynamic. It was just as important to understand my client's business as it was to understand my own.

Over time, my clients became friends. I built long-standing relationships that lasted 20, 30, even 40 years. That connection and trust made it a great job — one that I truly enjoyed every step of the way.

2. Satisfaction:

Satisfaction is the sense of fulfillment that comes from achieving your goals and making progress in your life and career. It's that feeling of pride and contentment you get when you look back on your accomplishments and recognize the effort and dedication that went into them. Satisfaction often comes from setting and achieving meaningful goals, both big and small. It's important to acknowledge your successes and celebrate the milestones along the way. This doesn't mean resting on your laurels — it means valuing what you've achieved and allowing yourself to feel good about it.

In a professional setting, satisfaction can come from many sources: completing a challenging project, receiving recognition from clients or colleagues, advancing to a new role, or simply knowing you gave it your all. Taking the time to reflect on your progress can deepen that sense of fulfillment and reinforce your passion for what you do.

Throughout my career, I worked in a mid-sized firm, then a large corporation, and eventually, I ran my own company. Each experience brought me tremendous satisfaction in different ways. My personal motto was always: “If you’re going to do something, do it well — do it to the best of your ability. You can’t do better than your best.”

That principle guided me and my team. Whenever we lost a bid for a new client or missed out on a big opportunity, I would always say: “If we can look ourselves in the mirror and honestly say we did our best, then we lost in the right way.” What drove me crazy was when we approached something half-heartedly and lost because we didn’t give it everything we had. That kind of loss — when you know you didn’t put your full heart into it — was hard to accept.

For me, true satisfaction came from knowing we gave our best effort and delivered high-quality work. And with that mindset, over the years, we won many new accounts and built lasting relationships.

You have to accept that in life, you win some and you lose some. The key is to win more than you lose — if you can do that, you come out ahead.

3. Meaningfulness:

Meaningfulness is perhaps the most profound element of happiness. It's the sense that what you're doing has purpose and significance beyond yourself. It connects your work — and your life — to something larger: whether it's making a positive impact on others, contributing to a cause you believe in, or pursuing a personal mission that gives your life direction. Finding meaning in your work is essential for long-term happiness. It fuels deeper motivation and helps carry you through tough times. When your work reflects your values and contributes to something greater than you, it becomes more than just a job — it becomes a calling. Over my 46-year career, I found deep meaning in helping others through difficult moments. I must have paid millions of dollars in insurance claims. Working for three of the largest brokerage firms in their respective areas, I was part of teams that paid out truly colossal amounts. I never tracked every single claim — but there were many, ranging from a client's damaged mobile phone to the sinking of an oil platform off the coast of Brazil.

And yet, no matter the size of the claim, each one mattered deeply to our clients. That's the nature of insurance — it's nothing more than a promise for the future. A promise that, should an unfortunate event occur, we will be there to help. Our clients placed their trust in us, in our expertise, and in our word. And when the event did happen, and we delivered on that promise — that's when the work truly mattered.

To me, there's no greater sense of purpose than that. Making a difference in the life of a client — even during some of their most difficult moments — brought great meaning to my own life. That trust, and the ability to honor it, is what made the work so fulfilling.

Meaningfulness can be found in many forms. For some, it's helping others. For others, it's creating something that lasts, or innovating in a field they love. Whatever your path, finding meaning in your work is one of the surest ways to build a life of purpose and happiness.

The effort to achieve happiness

While happiness is crucial to success, it doesn't come automatically. It requires conscious effort and self-awareness. Just as you would invest time and energy into developing your skills or building your business, you should also invest in your happiness. This might involve making changes to your work environment, seeking out activities that bring you joy, setting meaningful goals, or even reevaluating your career path to ensure it aligns with your values.

Studying and reading about happiness can also provide valuable insights and tools to help you cultivate it in your life. There are many excellent books and resources available that explore the science of happiness, offer practical advice, and share inspiring stories of those who have successfully integrated happiness into their careers. By dedicating time to understanding and pursuing happiness, you can create a more fulfilling and successful life.

The strategic importance of happiness

So, golden rule #17 — Find happiness — is a reminder that true success is not just about what you achieve, but how you feel along the way. Happiness is not a luxury; it is a necessity for anyone who wants to build a successful and sustainable career. By focusing on the three pillars of happiness — enjoyment, satisfaction, and meaningfulness — you can create a foundation for lasting success and fulfillment.

Remember, happiness is something you cultivate through conscious effort and intentional choices. It is not something that happens to you, but something you create.

As you pursue your career and personal goals, make sure that happiness is part of the equation. It will not only make your journey more enjoyable but will also enhance your ability to achieve your fullest potential.

Golden rule # 18
Physical, mental, and spiritual exercises

Maintaining balance in life is crucial, especially when pursuing a long and demanding career. While work and education often take center stage, it's essential to remember that physical, mental, and spiritual well-being are equally important. These aspects of life contribute not only to personal happiness but also to professional success. One of my biggest regrets is not maintaining my physical fitness during the 40 years I worked at A&P, A&A, Aon, and CredRisk Seguros.

Reflecting on this now, I realize how vital it is to nurture all aspects of oneself to achieve a fulfilling life.

The importance of physical exercise

In my school days, I was a fairly good athlete. I played on the rugby, hockey, and golf teams, and I enjoyed the sense of discipline, teamwork, and physical challenge that sports provided. However, as my career progressed, I allowed work and education to take precedence over my physical health. Like many professionals, I prioritized my career ambitions, often at the expense of my physical well-being. As a result, I drifted away from the physical activities that had once been a regular part of my life.

This year, I made the decision to get back into shape after 40 years of minimal physical activity. It's a commitment that requires patience and perseverance, and I know it will take a few years to regain the fitness level I had four decades ago. I've been exercising six days a week, gradually rebuilding my strength and stamina. While I may not yet consider myself a sportsman, I'm on a path that I believe will lead me back to a healthier, more active lifestyle.

If I could offer one piece of advice to young people, it would be this: by all means, study and continue learning throughout your career, but don't stop exercising. Physical fitness is not just about maintaining a certain appearance or athletic ability; it's about sustaining the energy and resilience needed to navigate the challenges of life and work. Regular exercise helps reduce stress, improves concentration, and enhances overall well-being, all of which are critical for sustained success in any field. Neglecting physical health can lead to regrets later in life, as it becomes increasingly difficult to regain lost fitness with age. Staying physically fit will help you work better and live better.

Mental exercise: sharpening the mind

Just as physical exercise is crucial for the body, mental exercise is essential for the mind. The demands of a career, particularly in fast-paced and intellectually challenging fields, require a sharp, agile mind. Keeping your mind active and engaged is not just about professional success; it's about maintaining cognitive health throughout your life.

Mental exercise can take many forms. Continuous learning, whether through formal education, reading, or engaging in new experiences, keeps the mind sharp and adaptable. It's important to challenge yourself regularly, whether by learning a new skill, solving complex problems, or engaging in creative activities. These activities stimulate the brain, encouraging neuroplasticity — the brain's ability to form new neural connections — which is vital for cognitive function as we age.

Moreover, mental exercise helps in maintaining focus and clarity in decision-making, which are crucial in both personal and professional settings. It allows you to approach problems with a fresh perspective, think critically, and make informed decisions. In a world that is constantly evolving, the ability to learn and adapt is more important than ever. By keeping your mind active, you ensure that you remain competitive and relevant in your field.

Spiritual exercise: finding meaning and balance

While physical and mental exercises are vital, spiritual exercise is equally important for achieving a balanced and fulfilling life. Spirituality doesn't necessarily mean religious practice; it's about connecting with something greater than oneself, finding purpose, and cultivating inner peace. For some, this may involve religious practices, while for others, it could mean meditation, mindfulness, or spending time in nature.

Spiritual exercise helps you maintain balance in life, offering a sense of calm and perspective that can be particularly valuable in the high-pressure world of business. It allows you to step back from the daily grind and reflect on what truly matters, helping you to align your actions with your values and purpose. This alignment is crucial for long-term happiness and fulfillment.

Incorporating spiritual practices into your daily routine can also enhance your emotional resilience. Life and work come with their share of challenges, and having a strong spiritual foundation can help you navigate these difficulties with grace and composure. Whether it's through meditation, prayer, or simply taking time each day to reflect on your goals and intentions, spiritual exercise nurtures the soul and provides the strength to face life's challenges with a positive mindset.

Achieving a balanced life

The key to a successful and fulfilling life lies in balancing physical, mental, and spiritual exercises. Neglecting any one of these aspects can lead to imbalances that affect your overall well-being and performance. For instance, focusing solely on your career without paying attention to your physical health can lead to burnout, while neglecting mental and spiritual well-being can result in a lack of clarity, purpose, and inner peace.

Achieving this balance requires conscious effort and discipline. It's about making time for exercise, continuing to challenge your mind, and nurturing your spirit, even when life gets busy. It's also about recognizing that these practices are interconnected—physical exercise can improve mental clarity, mental exercise can enhance your ability to engage in spiritual practices, and spiritual well-being can motivate you to take care of your body and mind.

The path to holistic success

As outlined above, golden rule #18 — Physical, mental, and spiritual exercises — highlights the importance of a holistic approach to life and career. Success is not just about professional achievements; it's about maintaining the health and well-being that allows you to enjoy and sustain that success over the long term. By committing to physical fitness, keeping your mind sharp, and nurturing your spirit, you create a foundation for a life that is not only successful but also fulfilling and balanced.

As I work to regain my physical fitness and continue to exercise my mind and spirit, I encourage others to do the same. Don't wait until later in life to realize the importance of these practices — start now and make them an integral part of your daily routine. In doing so, you'll not only enhance your career but also enrich your life in ways that go far beyond professional success.

In my own experience, I found it difficult to separate business hours from personal time. I devoted far too many hours to my work and my company — often at the expense of my well-being and my family's needs. It's an easy trap to fall into, which is why I strongly encourage readers to prioritize finding a healthy balance.

By aligning your professional commitments with meaningful time for your family, you'll be taking a crucial step toward greater happiness and a more fulfilling life.

Chapter Four

Why did I sell my company to MDS?

Given the success of CredRisk Seguros, you might wonder why I decided to sell the company to MDS. After all, we had built a highly profitable, well-respected business from the ground up. The decision to sell was far from easy; in fact, it was one of the most challenging decisions of my career. CredRisk Seguros was more than just a business to me — it was my fifth "child." I had nurtured it from its inception in 2007, starting with zero clients, and over the years, I "fed," "educated," "healed," and "clothed" this "child" until it became the market leader in trade credit insurance in Brazil.

The evolution of CredRisk Seguros

When I first established CredRisk Seguros, the concept of a mono-line, specialized trade credit insurance brokerage was relatively novel in Brazil. The idea was to focus intensely on one line of insurance and become the best in that field. From the clients' perspective, this turned out to be an exceptional idea. They received the best service in the market because our entire business model was designed around doing one thing exceptionally well. We didn't try to be everything to everyone; instead, we concentrated all our resources, expertise, and attention on trade credit insurance. This focus allowed us to offer unparalleled service and solutions, which our clients recognized and valued. No other firm in Brazil could match our level of specialization, and this became our competitive edge.

However, as the company grew and matured, I began to see potential risks in our business model. The very focus that had driven our success also made us vulnerable. Being a mono-line broker, offering only one product, meant that any significant changes in the market, local legislation, or the broader economic environment could have catastrophic consequences for us. This realization led me to take proactive steps to diversify our business.

In 2012, seeking to diversify my revenue streams, I partnered up with an experienced credit professional to establish an innovative credit consulting firm named CredPartner. Unlike traditional brokerage firms, CredPartner did not sell credit insurance. Instead, we mainly provided credit and collections consultancy services, developed state-of-the-art credit reports, and offered in-house training for our clients' employees. These services were offered on an hourly fee basis.

Although this company only contributed approximately 10% of our group's total annual revenues, this company added important complementary services and value to the overall organization as it became a key differentiator for our business. At the time, no other competitors in Brazil offered similar services, which gave us a significant edge and helped us win many new strategic accounts.

In 2016, I established a sister brokerage company focused on marine insurance. This move was designed to spread our business risk across two lines of insurance rather than relying solely on trade credit insurance. While this diversification provided some additional security, the underlying vulnerability of our specialized business model remained a concern.

The consolidation trend and acquisition proposals

Over the last two decades, the global business environment has seen a significant trend toward consolidation, with companies accelerating growth through acquisitions. The Brazilian insurance brokerage market has also experienced this trend, with large brokerage houses increasingly looking to acquire smaller, specialized firms like CredRisk Seguros. Almost every year, we were approached by several large brokers with acquisition offers. Despite the attractive terms, none of these proposals truly resonated with me. I wasn't interested in selling the company unless I could find a partner who would align with our values and vision for the future.

Then, in mid-2021, we were approached by MDS. This proposal was different from the others. It wasn't just about selling the company; it was about creating a strategic partnership that would benefit both parties. MDS operated in almost every line of insurance, except for trade credit insurance, where they lacked a significant presence. On the other hand, CredRisk Seguros was a market leader in trade credit insurance but needed to diversify its risk and become part of a larger organization with a broader range of products. The alignment of our needs made the MDS proposal compelling.

The strategic advantages of the MDS acquisition

The acquisition by MDS offered several strategic advantages. First, it allowed CredRisk Seguros to become part of a much larger organization with extensive resources and a broader product portfolio. This diversification significantly reduced the business risk associated with relying on a single product line. By integrating with MDS, we were able to offer our clients not just the best trade credit insurance services but also access to a wide range of other insurance products, enhancing the overall value proposition.

Moreover, the acquisition was a win-win situation for both companies. MDS instantly became the largest trade credit insurance broker in Brazil, leveraging our expertise and market position. At the same time, CredRisk Seguros gained the strength and stability of being part of the third-largest general insurance broker in Brazil. This merger created synergies that allowed both companies to grow and thrive in a competitive market.

The acquisition also brought significant benefits to our clients. They became part of the MDS family of companies, which shared the same work ethos and service standards they had come to expect from CredRisk Seguros. In addition, they now had access to a much stronger company with greater resources and a broader range of services at their disposal. This enhanced our ability to meet their needs and further solidified our relationships with them.

For our employees, the acquisition opened up new career opportunities. Working for a larger organization like MDS provided them with access to a global network of companies, expanding their professional horizons. The acquisition also created opportunities for cross-selling, allowing us to introduce our trade credit insurance products to MDS's existing client base of approximately

5,000 clients. This expanded our reach and allowed us to continue growing the business.

A thoughtful exit strategy

For the shareholders who had reached retirement age, the acquisition by MDS provided an ideal exit strategy. It allowed them to transition out of the business while ensuring that the company's reputation for excellence in service would continue under new ownership. The acquisition also mitigated the risks associated with operating a mono-line brokerage, providing peace of mind that CredRisk Seguros would continue to thrive in a changing market environment.

One of the most significant advantages of the acquisition was gaining access to the global Brokerslink network, which includes brokers spread across 133 countries with more than 10,000 collaborators. This global reach provided CredRisk Seguros with opportunities to expand its services internationally, tapping into new markets and clients.

The transition to MDS and future prospects

I have spent the last three years of my career working for MDS in the São Paulo office. It has been a pleasure to work with such a fine group of professionals at MDS. Despite an unfavorable macroeconomic environment, we have continued to grow the trade credit business. This growth is a testament to the strength of the MDS-CredRisk partnership and the commitment of our team to delivering exceptional service to our clients. One of my primary objectives during these last three years has been to ensure a smooth management transition to a younger team. This team was handpicked and thoroughly trained, and I have had the privilege of watching, with great satisfaction, how competently they have taken over the reins. The management transition has already taken place, and I am confident that this young team will take the trade credit business to even greater heights in the coming years — beyond what I could have imagined. In conclusion, the decision to sell CredRisk Seguros to MDS was not taken lightly. It was a strategic move that allowed the company to continue growing and thriving in a rapidly changing market. While it was difficult to part with a business that I had nurtured for fifteen years, I am confident that the decision was the right one for our clients, employees, and shareholders. The acquisition by MDS has positioned CredRisk Seguros for continued success, ensuring that the legacy we built will endure for years to come.

Closing remarks

As I bring this book to a close, I hope that the four-phase career plan and the 18 golden rules I've shared have provided you with not only valuable insights but also the motivation to set and pursue your personal and professional objectives. Remember, the key to success lies in clarity of purpose. Take the time to put your objectives and plans in writing and make it a habit to review and revise them regularly. This disciplined approach will keep you focused and ensure that you're always moving in the right direction.

Tracking your achievements is just as important as setting goals. Celebrate your victories, no matter how small, because they are the milestones that mark your progress. However, one critical piece of advice I want to leave you with is this: avoid the trap of comparing yourself to others. In today's world, it's easy to fall into the cycle of comparison, but it's a path that leads to dissatisfaction and frustration.

There will always be someone with more wealth, a larger home, or a more luxurious lifestyle. But these external markers are not true measures of success. Instead, focus on your own journey and compare the "you" of today against the "you" of a year ago. Strive for continuous improvement in all areas of your life, and you'll find that this approach brings you greater happiness and fulfillment.

In your professional life, work diligently to contribute to the growth of your organization, particularly in terms of profitability. To achieve this, innovation is key. Always seek to enhance Best Practices — find ways to do things better, faster, and more cost-effectively. The professionals who make a lasting impact are those who add value to their work and drive transformation within their companies. Aim to be that person who changes things for the better, and you will find your work not only fulfilling but also meaningful.

Remember, careers are more like marathons than 100-meter sprints. They require careful planning, dedication, and sustained effort over time. It's not just about working hard at your job; it's about working just as hard on yourself. Personal development is the foundation of professional success. To improve in your career, you must also strive to improve personally. Never stop learning. Take every opportunity to expand your knowledge, whether through courses, workshops, or self-study. And above all, never stop reading. Books offer us a window into new ideas, perspectives, and solutions to the challenges we face in life and work.

Consider this book an introduction — a starting point for your journey. The golden rules I've shared are principles that have guided me throughout my career, and I encourage you to explore them further.

Seek out additional resources, dive deeper into the topics that resonate with you, and continue to build your knowledge and skills.

If you find yourself in a place where your career has stalled, where you're unhappy, or where your financial situation isn't what you'd like it to be, I urge you to take action. Change is within your power. It's far easier for you to change than to wait for the world to change for you. You should be in control of your life, steering it in the direction you want it to go. If necessary, hire a coach or a mentor to help you regain focus and momentum. And if a coach or mentor isn't accessible to you, start by applying the four-phase career plan and the 18 golden rules outlined in this book. They worked for me, and I believe they can work for you too. What do you have to lose?

Finally, I want to express my deepest gratitude to José Manuel Dias da Fonseca, Global CEO of MDS, and Ariel Couto, CEO of MDS Brazil. Their outstanding leadership and friendship over the last three years have been invaluable to me. I have no doubt that their success is due, in large part, to the fact that they have embodied many of the golden rules mentioned in this book, especially golden rule #4 — To be a gentleman. Their example has been a source of inspiration, and I hope that the lessons shared in this book will inspire you in your journey as well.

Thank you for taking the time to read this book. I wish you all the best in your pursuit of success, happiness, and fulfillment. Remember, the journey is yours to shape, and with the right principles guiding you, there are no limits to what you can achieve.

A summary of the 18 golden rules

1. You don't want to be the biggest... you want to be the richest.
2. Successful managers must be lazy and intelligent.
3. You can't change the world... but you can change yourself.
4. Be a gentleman.
5. Work harder on yourself than on your job.
6. Network as much as possible.
7. Keep ahead of the market.
8. Differentiate yourself from the crowd.
9. Be persistent... never give up... fight to the end.
10. Remove fear from your mind.
11. "Genius is 1% inspiration and 99% perspiration" - Thomas Edison
12. Take risks.
13. Be a reference in your field of business.
14. Surround yourself with people who are better than you.
15. Keep improving Best Practices.
16. Be the "go-to" person in your organization.
17. Find happiness.
18. Keep physically, mentally and spiritually fit.

About the Author

Phillip Krinker

Phillip Krinker launched his insurance career in 1978 at Adams & Porter in São Paulo, beginning a journey that would see him become one of the most innovative figures in Brazil's insurance industry. In 1994, he moved to Alexander & Alexander, which later became part of Aon Risk Services, before taking a bold leap in 2007 by founding CredRisk Seguros. This company would go on to become one of Brazil's first specialized trade credit insurance brokerage firms, dedicated solely to navigating this complex yet rewarding niche.

Over the course of 46 years, Phillip didn't just work across various lines of insurance — he revolutionized them. He consistently introduced cutting-edge insurance products and services, helping to shape the future of the Brazilian market.

In the 1990s, when President Fernando Henrique Cardoso initiated Brazil's ambitious privatization program, Phillip saw an unprecedented opportunity. He swiftly established a "Privatization Department" to manage the intricate risks associated with newly privatized industries like railroads, airports, and ports.

Through his leadership, he imported and tailored innovative insurance solutions that reshaped how these sectors safeguarded their assets.

Building on this success, Phillip spearheaded the creation of a "Financial Lines Department," developing expertise in Directors & Officers (D&O) Insurance, Errors & Omissions (E&O) Insurance, Surety and Bonds, and Trade Credit Insurance — each one designed to meet the growing demands of the modern business landscape.

But it was Trade Credit Insurance that truly captured Phillip's passion. In 2007, driven by the complex nature of trade credit policies and the advanced risk management techniques that help businesses manage credit risks before transferring them to insurers, Phillip founded CredRisk Seguros. He realized that only a focused, specialized brokerage could offer the proactive, expert service necessary to protect clients and defend their interests.

Trade Credit Insurance became a game changer. It didn't just reduce credit risk; it empowered businesses to confidently expand into new markets and increase their credit exposure to existing clients without risking dangerous concentrations of credit risks.

By 2022, CredRisk Seguros had become Brazil's premier trade credit insurance broker. Phillip's clients no longer viewed insurance premiums as a mere cost — they saw them as an investment in their growth and security. This shift in perception marked a crowning achievement in Phillip's career, bringing him immense professional fulfillment.